You're on Your Way
to an
Amazing Future

Copyright © 2020 by Heather Stillufsen.

All rights reserved. No part of this publication may be reproduced, stored in a retrieval system or transmitted in any form or by any means, electronic, mechanical, photocopying, recording or otherwise, without the written permission of the publisher.

ISBN: 978-1-68088-343-5

█ and Blue Mountain Press are registered in U.S. Patent and Trademark Office. Certain trademarks are used under license.

Printed in China.
Second Printing: 2021

♻ This book is printed on recycled paper.

This book is printed on paper that has been specially produced to be acid free (neutral pH) and contains no groundwood or unbleached pulp. It conforms with the requirements of the American National Standards Institute, Inc., so as to ensure that this book will last and be enjoyed by future generations.

Blue Mountain Arts, Inc.
P.O. Box 4549, Boulder, Colorado 80306

You're on Your Way to an
to an
Amazing Future

Written and Illustrated by
Heather Stillufsen

Blue Mountain Press™
Boulder, Colorado

You're on your way
to an amazing *future*...
where *nothing* is impossible!
Your door of opportunity
is out there waiting
to be *opened*.

Take the time to *think* about
what you truly want in life.
Commit to your goals.
Make a plan, and go after it
with all your heart.
Work hard, do your *best*,
and *never* give up!

No matter where you
may be on your *journey*,
be glad for where you have been
and where you are going.
Look at all you have
accomplished.
Take a moment to *smile*
and reflect on your success
so far.
And most of all…
be proud of *you!*

Six Things to Remember
as You Make Your *Mark*
on the World:

- Be yourself
- *Accept* yourself
- Nourish yourself
- *Challenge* yourself
- Be good to yourself
- *Treat* yourself with kindness

Life is *filled* with lessons
we learn along the way.
Sometimes we get them right,
and sometimes we don't.
It's *okay* to stumble
and make mistakes.
Take it as a lesson learned.
Move on and keep going.

No one is perfect.
Our *imperfections*
make us who we are.
So celebrate your *uniqueness*,
and go out and be beautiful,
one-of-a-kind you!

THE
BEGIN...

CHA...
ON...

CHAPTER
TWO

Hearts

change

friendship

HEARTACHE

school

LOVE

you and me

Remember that *you* are in charge
of your own story.
It's up to *you* and only *you*
to write it as you wish
and live it as you want.
Your story is still unfolding,
so go ahead and turn the page…
Your next chapter is waiting.

You must *continually* believe in yourself, even when others don't. You are *capable* of so very much. Do not give up on your dreams or your hopes… *ever.*

Have *patience*.
It may take some time to
reach your goals.
You may be scared about
what lies ahead,
but keep up the hard work.
You will get there.
Remember... good things
take time.

Surround yourself with
positive, supportive people…
people who will *lift* you up
and stand by your side
through the good days
and the bad days too…
people who will *inspire* you,
listen to you,
be there for you,
and recognize the good in you.
These are the people who will
bring something *special*
to your world.

A Few Words of *Advice*…

- ♥ Don't ever let what's bothering you… get the *best* of you
- ♥ Be true to yourself
- ♥ *Respect* people
- ♥ Be grateful
- ♥ Help others
- ♥ If you don't like your situation… *change* it!

Happiness belongs to you!

You're
on your
way
to
great things

What is it that you *love* to do?
Do you love art?
Do you love yoga, writing,
drawing, working out,
cooking, reading,
making numbers work together,
finance, law, teaching others?
Let that be what you do *more* of...

Have the courage to go out
and follow your passions.
Live your dream...
and let what you love
be what you do!

Just a thought...
be grateful
be present
be interested

If you ever feel like
giving up,
know that it's going
to get better.
Things don't stay the same forever.
Think *positive* and know
that this is all part
of your journey.
Every little piece of *today*
is making you into
who you will be *tomorrow.*

Growth comes
from stepping outside of
your *comfort zone.*
Let go of fear and self-doubt…
It's *your* time to blossom.

The *future* is about to
open up to you.
So embrace the excitement,
accept the challenges…
and *always* keep a bit of home
tucked in your *heart*.

How to Make the *Most* of Every Day:

- Have *courage*
- Adopt an attitude of gratitude
- *Follow* your passions
- Fill your life with what brings you *joy*
- Always look on the bright side
- Know there are *lessons* in every situation
- Focus on the good
- Enjoy the little things
- *Dream*

Your *potential* has no limit!
You can reach every single *goal*
you set out to achieve
when you put your mind to it.

You are smart, worthy,
kind, beautiful, and *strong*...
and yes, you *can*
handle anything
that comes your way.
Now *go out* and
show the world!

About the Author

Heather Stillufsen fell in love with drawing as a child and has been holding a pencil ever since. She is best known for her delicate and whimsical illustration style, which has become instantly recognizable. From friendship to family to fashion, Heather's art demonstrates a contemporary sensibility for

Photo by Christine E. Allen

people of all ages. Her words are written from the heart and offer those who read them the hope of a brighter day and inspiration to live life to the fullest.

Heather is the author of six books: *Sisters Make Life More Beautiful, Mothers and Daughters Are Connected by the Heart, May Your Holidays Be Merry and Bright, Life Is Tough… but So Are You, Best Friends Make the Best Memories,* and *You're on Your Way to an Amazing Future.*

Her refreshing and elegant illustrations can also be found on calendars, planners, journals, greeting cards, art prints, hand-painted needlepoint canvases, and more.

She currently lives in New Jersey with her husband, two daughters, and German Shorthaired Pointer.